51 things to make with

Egg
Boxes

Fiona Hayes

QED

Contents

Basic Equipment

Most of these projects use some or all of the following equipment, so keep these handy:

- **PVA glue**
- **Scissors**
- **Pencils**
- **Ruler**
- **Felt-tip pens**
- **Paint brushes**

Unless specified, short, six-egg boxes that have hinges on the long side are used.

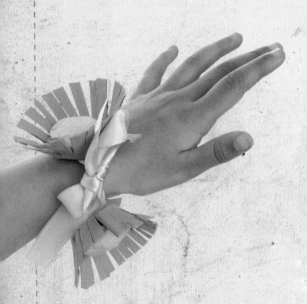

Cute Chicken

This cute chicken is the perfect egg-holder! Make a row of these clucky cuties – they'll brighten up any kitchen.

1

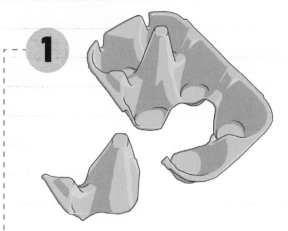

Cut the corner from the base of an egg box. Paint your chicken white or brown.

2

Fold a small piece of red card in half. Cut out a half-heart shape. You will need to make two of these – one for the chicken's comb and one for its wattles.

3

comb

wattles

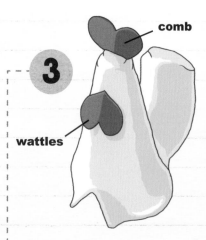

Glue the comb and wattles to the body, as shown above.

4

Using the same method you used in step 2, cut out a triangular beak.

5

Glue the beak in place. Add some googly eyes.

6

Why not make a row of chickens from one long egg box? You could keep all your Easter eggs in it!

Roaring Lion Hand Puppet

Who knew you could make a lion from an egg box? Your friends will go WILD when they see it!

1

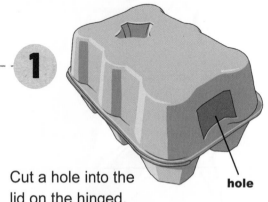

hole

Cut a hole into the lid on the hinged, short side of the egg box. The hole should be big enough to fit two fingers inside.

2

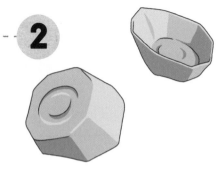

Cut two bowls from the base of another egg box. Trim the sides to give them a sloped edge.

3

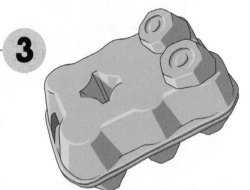

Glue the bowls to the top of the first box. They will be the eyes. Paint the lion's head yellow.

4

Cut slits in a strip of brown felt or card for the mane. You may need two pieces to make a thick mane.

5

Glue the mane to the head.

6

Cut ears from the white card, paint yellow and glue into position.

7

Add some googly eyes.

8

To make your lion roar, put two fingers in the dip on its head and two fingers in the hole at the back of its head and your thumb under the box. Pull up the lid and hear it...

Handy Hint

If you can't find egg boxes with hinges on the short side, cut off the lid of a regular egg box and make paper hinges on the short side.

ROAR

Bee

Get buzzing and make a pretty bumblebee!

You will need

One egg box

Yellow, black, blue and white paint

White and blue card

Two yellow bendy straws

Two googly eyes

1 Paint the top of your box yellow and the bottom black. Add black stripes to the top.

2 At one end of the box, use a pencil to make two holes. Cut the bendy part off two straws and insert into the holes.

3 Cut out two wings from white card. Paint veins on the wings, then glue into position. Paint a mouth onto your bee.

4 Add blue circles of card behind the eyes to make them stand out. Glue the eyes to the blue circles and then to the egg box. Buzz, buzz, your bee is ready!

Hedgehog

This hedgehog is so adorable all your friends will want to make one.

1

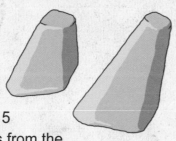

Cut out 12–15 pointed parts from the bottom of an egg box. Trim the bottoms so they are slightly angled.

2

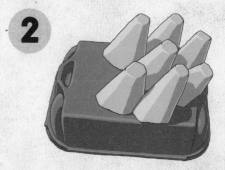

Glue the parts onto one end of an egg box. Allow the parts on the top to dry before you glue parts to the sides.

3

Once the glue is dry, paint the top of the body and spikes brown, and the rest yellow.

4

Cut a bowl from the base of an egg box, paint it yellow. Glue it to the head, to make a snout. Use a bottle top for the nose. Glue it to the snout. Add circles of felt, then add the eyes. Your hedgehog is now ready to snuffle about!

Barking Dog Hand Puppet

You will need

Two egg boxes
(one must have hinges
on the short side)

**Brown, black and
red paint**

Brown and black felt

Two googly eyes

1

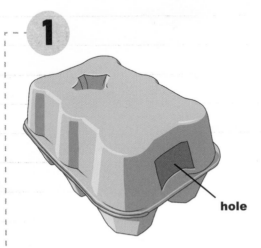

hole

Cut a hole into the lid on the hinged, short side of the egg box. The hole should be big enough to fit two fingers inside.

2

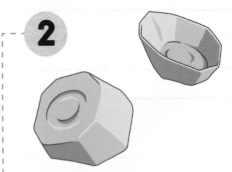

Cut two bowls from the base of another box. Trim the sides to give them a sloped edge.

3

Glue the bowls to the top of the box. They will be the dog's eyes.

4

Now paint your dog. Don't forget to paint the inside of its mouth red!

5

Cut a pair of ears and a nose from felt.

6

Glue in place.

7

Add some googly eyes.

8

To make your dog bark, put two fingers in the dip on its head, two fingers in the hole at the back of its head and your thumb under the box. Pull up the lid.

WOOF
WOOF

Dragon

This red-hot dragon will fire up your egg-box crafty collection.

1

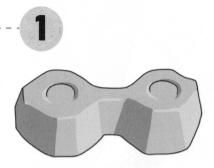

For the eyes, cut a two-bowl section from the bottom of an egg box.

2

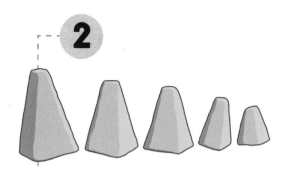

For the tail, cut six pointed parts from the bottom of another egg box. Make the parts different sizes.

3

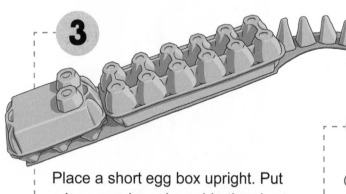

Place a short egg box upright. Put a long egg box alongside the short one, but upside-down. Position the tail spikes to form the tail. Now cut a piece of card the same length as your dragon. Cut a curve into the card, to shape the tail. Then glue all the parts onto the card, as shown.

4

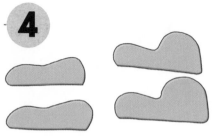

Cut out four legs from the thick card and glue them onto the body, as shown in step 5.

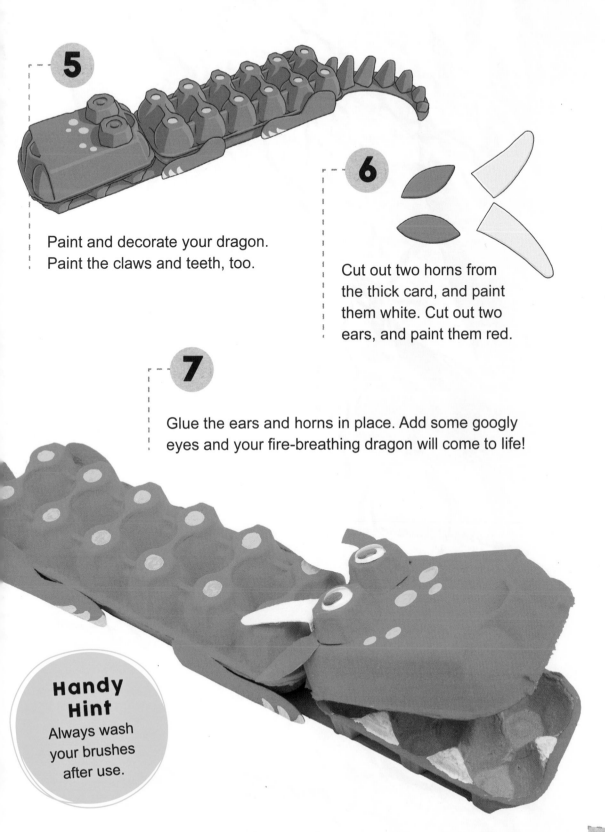

5

Paint and decorate your dragon. Paint the claws and teeth, too.

6

Cut out two horns from the thick card, and paint them white. Cut out two ears, and paint them red.

7

Glue the ears and horns in place. Add some googly eyes and your fire-breathing dragon will come to life!

Handy Hint
Always wash your brushes after use.

Dumper Truck

1

Cut the small egg box in two, as shown. The large section will be the cab.

2

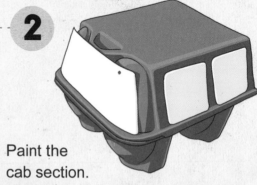

Paint the cab section. Cut out some windows from white card, and draw on passengers. Glue the windows in place.

3

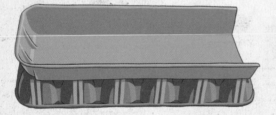

Cut the lid off a long egg box. Turn it upside-down and glue onto the egg box base. Paint the wagon.

4

Cut a piece of thick card the length of the cab and wagon. Then glue them onto the card.

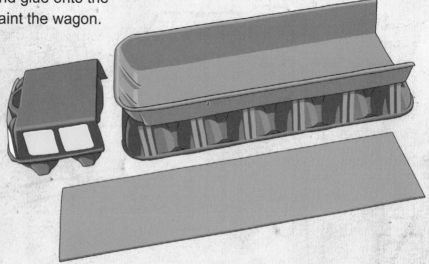

5

Cut out
eight circles
for the wheels
and paint them.

6

Glue the wheels onto
the cab and wagon.

Handy Hint

Use clothes pegs to
hold pieces in place
while waiting for
them to dry.

7

Add two bottle tops to
the cab, for hazard lights.
Your truck is ready!

VROOM

VROOM

Fairy Magic

Do you love fairies? You certainly will once you've made this pretty little fairy!

1

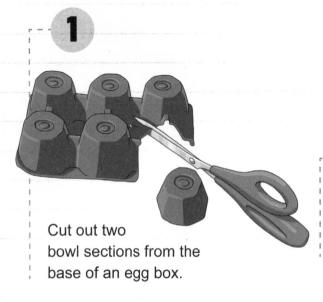

Cut out two bowl sections from the base of an egg box.

2

Glue the bowls together to make a barrel.

3

Glue on the polystyrene ball. Paint the ball and the bowls. For the hair, glue on some wool.

4

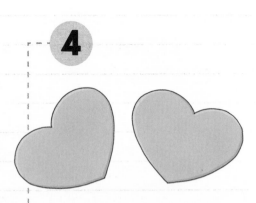

For the wings, cut out two hearts from felt or card.

5

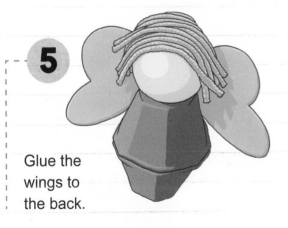

Glue the wings to the back.

6

Draw on some eyes and a friendly smile and your fairy is ready to wave her magic wand!

Handy Hint

Make a few of these magical fairies so that you have an entire fairy kingdom.

Fire Engine

Save the day by making this amazing fire engine. You could make two so that you have your very own fire station!

You will need

Two egg boxes

Thick card

Red, white, blue and yellow paint

The tops of two toothpaste tubes

Three straws

Shiny corrugated card

1

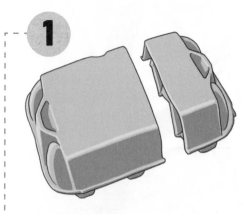

Cut an egg box in two, as shown. The large section will be the cab.

2

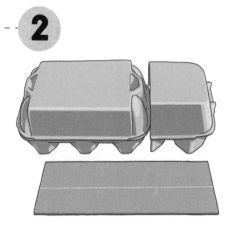

Glue the cab and another egg box to a piece of thick card.

3

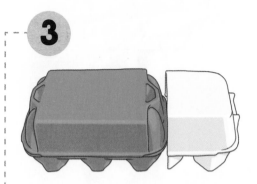

Paint the back section red, and the front part white. When the paint is dry, add some blue windows.

4

Cut out six circles from the thick card for the wheels. Paint and glue in place. Glue two tube tops to the top of the cab.

5

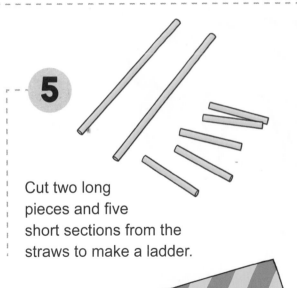

Cut two long pieces and five short sections from the straws to make a ladder.

6

Glue the ladder to the top of the truck.

7

Make a hazard sign from thick card for the front of the truck, as shown.

8

Glue a piece of shiny corrugated card to the truck's side. Your fire engine is ready to zoom in to action!

NEE-NAW NEE-NAW

Funny Frog

What's bright green, very cute and will make a really big splash? This friendly little frog!

1

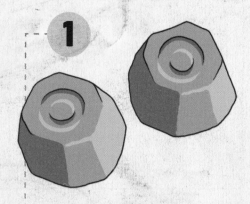

Cut two bowls from the base of an egg box. These will be the frog's eyes.

2

Cut the second egg box in two, as shown. The large part will be the body.

3

Cut the frog's legs from the lid of the small section.

4

Glue the frog's eyes and legs into position.

5

Paint the frog dark green, with a light green tummy.

Handy Hint

Let the paint dry completely before adding the spots.

6

Paint on some yellow spots and a red mouth. Add googly eyes, and, boing, your frog will leap away!

RIBBET

RIBBET

Happy Hippo

You will need

Three egg boxes
Pink and white paint
Thick card
Two googly eyes

1

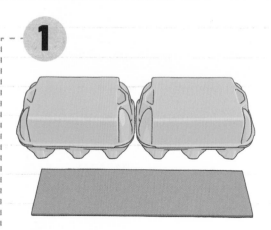

Glue two egg boxes onto
a piece of thick card.

2

Cut six bowls from the
base of another egg box.

3

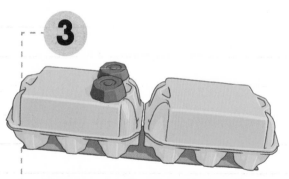

Glue two bowls onto the head
to make the hippo's eyes.

4

For the feet, glue the
remaining four bowls onto the
base. Paint the hippo pink.

5

Add spots, toenails and googly
eyes to the hippo. Paint the
inside of the mouth orange
and the teeth white. Cut two
tusks from the thick card
and glue them to the
front of the mouth.

Tortoise

You will need

Two egg boxes
Green and yellow paint
White card
Two googly eyes

1

Cut four bowls from the base of an egg box.

2

Glue two of the bowls to the top of an upturned egg box.

3

Paint the remaining two bowls yellow, then cut them in half. These will be the tortoise's feet.

4

Glue the feet in place.

5

Paint the egg box green, with yellow circles or spots. This will be the tortoise's shell.

6

Cut out a circle from card and paint it yellow. Glue this to the front of the shell. Add googly eyes and a smile to complete your cute little friend.

Christmas Tree

It's Christmas time! Fill your house with festive cheer by making this pretty little tree.

You will need

Three egg boxes

Green, red and yellow paint

Thick card

Shiny card

Ribbon

1

Draw a large triangle onto a thick piece of card. Add a pot shape to the bottom. Cut out.

2

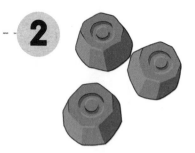

Cut around 15 bowls from the base of the egg boxes.

3

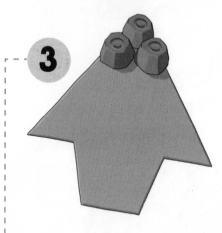

Glue the bowls to the top of the tree, so they fit together snuggly.

4

Cover the tree with bowls, but leave the pot section uncovered. Leave to dry.

5

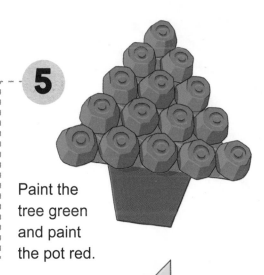

Paint the
tree green
and paint
the pot red.

6

Cut out lots
of circles from
shiny card, to make baubles.
Glue them onto your tree.

7

Cut out a star
from thick card,
and paint it yellow.

8

Glue the star to the top of
your tree. Attach a loop
of ribbon to the back of
the tree, so you can hang
it up at Christmas time.

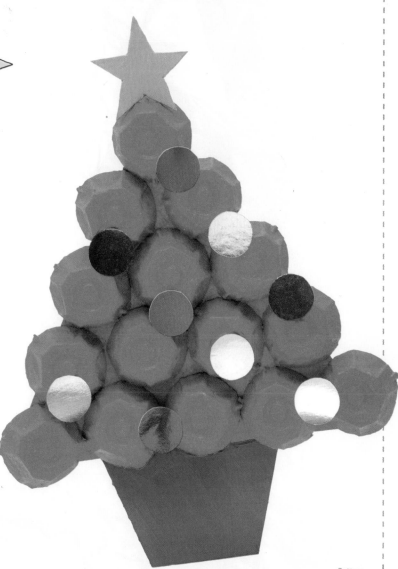

Handy Hint
You can make this
tree as large as you
like – you just need
lots of egg boxes!

Snowman

Brrrr! If it's cold outside, stay
indoors and make this perfect
snowman – it will never melt!

You will need

One egg box
White and black paint
Red felt
Thick orange card

1 Cut four bowls from the
base of an egg box.

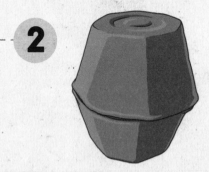

2 Glue two bowls together,
to make a barrel.

3 Glue on another bowl,
to make the head.

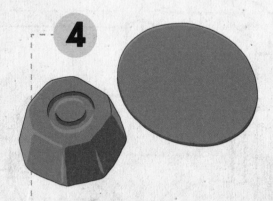

4 Cut a circle from the
lid of the egg box and
glue the remaining
bowl to the middle
of it to make a hat.

5

Paint the body white and the hat black.

6

Glue the hat in place. Tie a thin strip of felt around the neck for a scarf.

7

Add a little orange triangle for a carrot nose. Draw on some dots for eyes and a smile. Your super snowman is ready, come rain or shine!

Handy Hint

To make a circle, draw around a jar lid on card.

BRRRR

Mushrooms

You will need

Two egg boxes
White and red paint

1

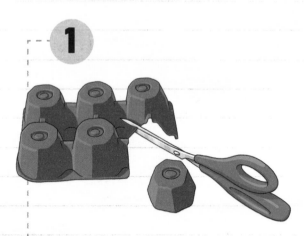

Cut the bowls from the base of an egg box.

2

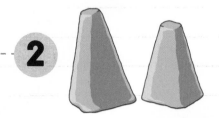

Cut out the pointed parts from the base of another egg box.

3

Paint the pointed parts white and the bowls red, with white spots.

4

Glue the bowls to the pointed parts. Arrange them to make a pretty woodland scene.

Sheep

**Make one sheep
or a whole flock!**

You will need

Three egg boxes   Thick card

White and black
paint   Pink felt or card

Two googly eyes

1

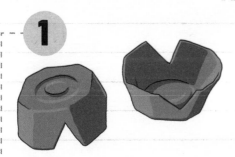

Cut four bowls from the base of an
egg box. Cut V-shaped notches
into the sides of the bowls.

2

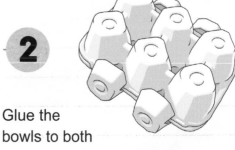

Glue the
bowls to both
sides of an upside-down egg
box, as shown. Paint it white.

3

Cut four bowls from the base
of another egg box for the
feet. Paint them black.

4

Cut out a head
from thick card,
and paint black.

5

Glue the head and legs
into position. Add a pink
nose, some googly eyes
and a cute smile to finish
your sheep...

BAA

29

Bird Mask

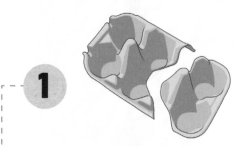

You will need

One egg box
Brown and yellow paint
White felt
Elastic

1 Cut the end section from the base of an egg box.

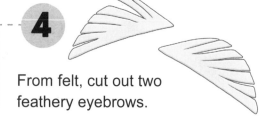

2 To make eyes, press a pencil into the egg box, as shown. Trim any rough edges.

3 Turn over the box, then cut a slit in the beak. Paint the head brown and the beak yellow.

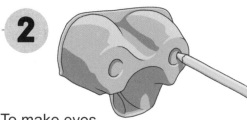

4 From felt, cut out two feathery eyebrows.

5 Glue the eyebrows in place.

6 With a pencil, make a small hole either side of the beak. Thread a piece of elastic through the holes. Tie a knot at each end to hold it in position. Your mask is ready.

Bracelet

You could make this lovely bracelet for yourself or give it to a friend as a pretty present.

You will need

One egg box
Pink paint
Yellow tissue paper
Ribbon

1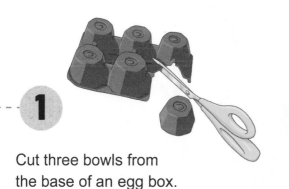
Cut three bowls from the base of an egg box.

2
Paint the bowls. Cut slits around the edges.

3
Scrunch up some yellow tissue paper and glue it into the centre of the bowls.

4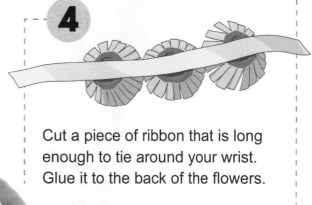
Cut a piece of ribbon that is long enough to tie around your wrist. Glue it to the back of the flowers.

5
Your bracelet is ready. Tie it around your wrist and finish with a pretty bow.

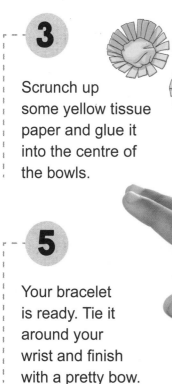

Octopus

Turn your bedroom into a watery wonderland by making this cute and colourful octopus.

1

Cut two bowls from the base of an egg box.

2

Glue the bowls to the top of an egg box, for the eyes.

3

Cut the bottom discs from the other egg boxes, for the suckers.

4

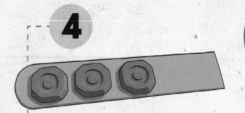

Cut out eight legs from thick card. Glue the suckers to the legs.

5

Paint the box a bright colour, and add some contrasting spots.

6

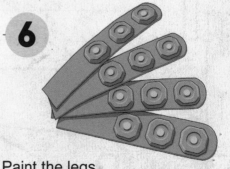

Paint the legs to match the body.

7

Open the egg box and glue the legs into position. Close the box.

8

Add some googly eyes. Watch out for those eight octopus legs!

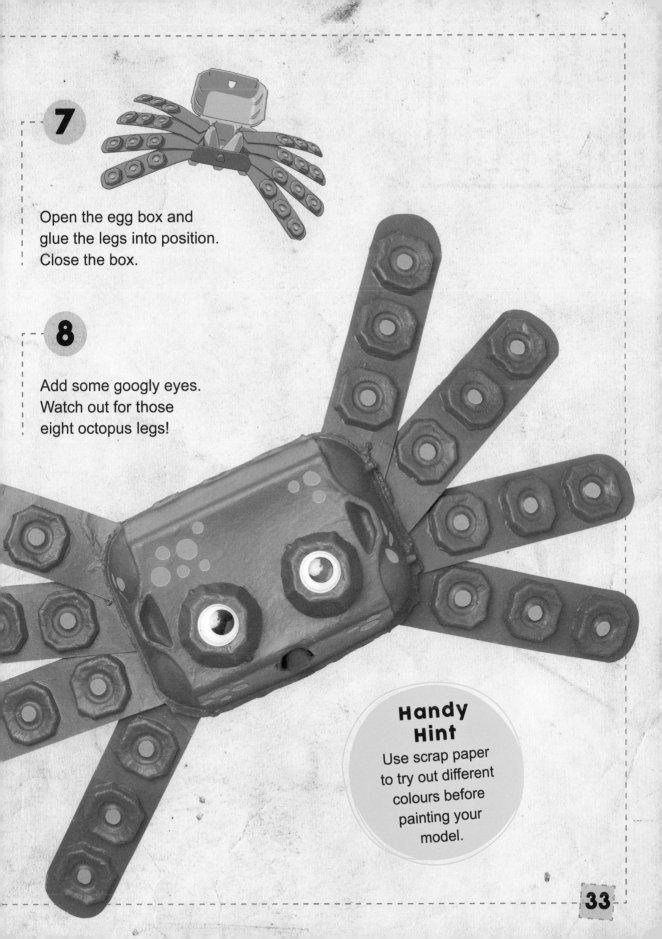

Handy Hint

Use scrap paper to try out different colours before painting your model.

Loveable Owl

Twit twoo! I can see you! Make this gorgeous little owl to watch over you all night long.

You will need

Two egg boxes
Thick card
Paint, including yellow paint
Two googly eyes

1

Cut the end from an egg box.

2

Cut two bowls from the base of another egg box.

3

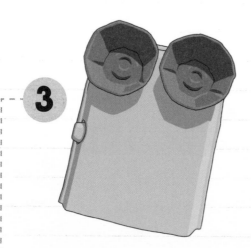

Glue the bowls to the front of the box, for the owl's eyes.

4

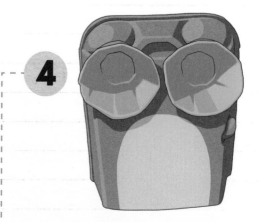

Paint the owl. Paint the eye sockets a contrasting colour, so they really stand out.

5

Cut out two wings from the thick card, and paint them to match the body.

6

Glue the wings and googly eyes in place.

7

Cut out a card triangle and paint it yellow. This is the beak. Fold it in half and glue in place. Your wise owl is ready to fly!

TWIT TWOO

Necklace

1

Cut 10 bowls from the base of two egg boxes.

2

Glue the bowls together to make barrel-shaped beads.

3

Paint the beads. Using a pencil, make a hole from one end of each bead to the other.

4

Glue a thin strip of card around the middle of each bead. This will hide the joins.

5

Cut a length of ribbon, attach it to a straw and thread it through the beads.

6

Tie the ends of the ribbon together. Your pretty necklace is ready to wear.

Bunny

You will need

Two egg boxes
Card
Paint
Pink and purple felt
Two googly eyes

1

Cut the end from an egg box.

2

Cut out two long ears from card.

3

Glue the ears to the top of the egg box.

4

Cut two corners from the top of another egg box. They will be feet.

5

Glue the feet in place. Paint your bunny.

6

Add a nose using a small piece of felt. Glue googly eyes onto two circles of felt to finish this cheeky chap!

Butterfly

1 Fold the paper in half and cut out a heart shape with a flat bottom, as shown. This will be your template.

You will need

Piece of paper
Two egg boxes
Paint
Thick card
Two googly eyes
Two bendy straws
Ribbon

2 Unfold the template. Draw around it on the thick card and cut out.

3 Cut out a line of three bowls from the base of an egg box.

4 Cut out the base of some egg box bowls, to decorate the wings.

5 Paint all the pieces and glue into position, as shown.

6 Cut the bendy piece from two straws, and glue to the back of the head. Add some googly eyes. Glue a piece of ribbon to the back of the butterfly to hang it up.

Caterpillar Pencil Holder

1

Cut the bowls from the base of an egg box.

2

Glue two bowls together, to make a barrel. Make six barrels.

3

Paint the barrels bright colours. Cut a strip of thick card, paint it green and then glue your barrels onto it.

4

Use a pencil to make a hole in the top of five barrels. Leave the end barrel.

5

Make two small holes in the top of the end barrel. Insert two pieces of bendy straw. Glue googly eyes onto circles of felt, and add a smile. Place your pencils in the holes – your pencil holder is ready!

Flower Garland

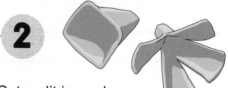

1

Cut the pointed parts from the bottom of an egg box.

2

Cut a slit in each corner of the pointed parts. Bend the four corners outwards.

3

Cut the edges into a petal shape. Paint them and leave to dry. Glue one pointed part onto another to make a flower. Repeat steps 1 to 3 to make as many flowers as you like.

4

Make a small hole in the middle of a flower. Thread through a piece of string.

5

Tie a knot in the string, as shown, then thread on your next flower.

6

Repeat step 5 until you have threaded on all your flowers. Tie a knot under the last flower. Decorate your bedroom with your beautiful flower garland.

Snails

Blaze a trail with these snails – all your friends will want one!

1 Cut two bowls from the base of an egg box. They will make the shell.

2 Cut out a long triangle from thick card. This will be the body. Paint the body and the shell pieces.

3 Glue the shell pieces onto either side of the body. Hold in place with an elastic band until dry.

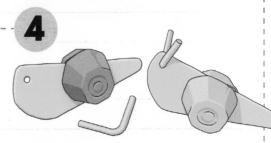

4 Cut a straw so the bendy part is in the middle. Make a hole in the body with a pencil. Insert the straw and bend upwards.

5 Repeat steps 1 to 4 to make another snail. Add spots or stripes to the shell, googly eyes and a smile. Why not make a set and line them up!

Flower Wreath

This beautiful flower wreath will brighten up a dull, rainy day and add some springtime colour to your home.

You will need

Three or more egg boxes

Paint, including green

Thick card

Tissue paper

Ribbon

1

Draw a large circle onto a piece of thick card. Draw a smaller circle inside. Cut out the large circle. Use a pencil to make a hole for your scissors, then cut out the middle circle to make a ring. Paint it green.

2

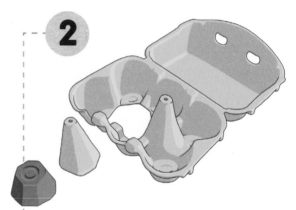

Cut the bowls and pointed parts from the bottom of the egg boxes.

3

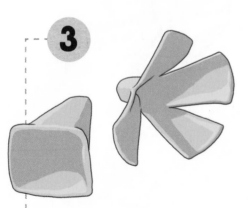

Cut a slit in each corner of the pointed parts. Bend the four corners outwards.

4

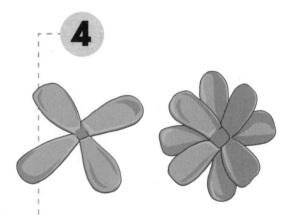

Cut the edges into a petal shape. Paint them. When they are dry, glue one pointed part onto another.

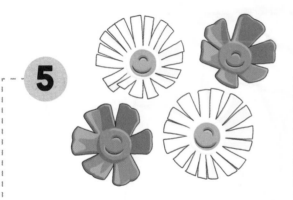

5

To make other types of flower, cut slits along the sides of the bowls, either close together or far apart, and bend outwards. Paint lots of different colours.

6

Cut some leaves from the thick card and paint them green. When the leaves and flowers are all dry, glue your flowers onto the ring.

7

Scrunch up some small pieces of tissue paper and glue in the centres of the flowers. Glue a piece of ribbon to the back of the garland. Find a spot in your home to hang your flower wreath – why not try one on your bedroom door?

Fox Mask

Be cunningly crafty and make this super-smart fox mask!

You will need

One egg box

Orange, white, black and pink paint

Card

Elastic

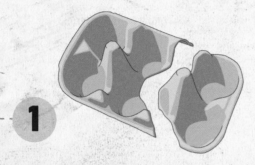

1 Cut the end section from the base of an egg box, as shown.

2 To make the eyes, press a pencil into the egg box, as shown. Trim any rough edges.

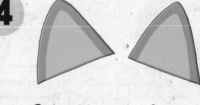

3 Turn over the box. Paint the top part orange, and the bottom part white. Add a black nose.

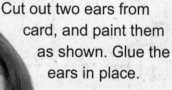

4 Cut out two ears from card, and paint them as shown. Glue the ears in place.

5 Make a small hole either side of the nose with a pencil. Thread elastic through the holes. Tie a knot at each end to hold it in position.

Cute Noses

You will need

One egg box

Yellow, pink, grey and black paint

Black card

Elastic

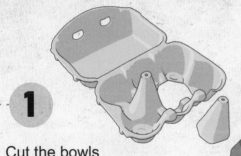

1

Cut the bowls and the pointed parts from the base of an egg box.

2

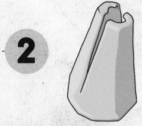

Use a pointed part to make a beak. Cut a slit in it and paint yellow.

3

You can make a piglet's nose from a bowl. Paint it pink and add some nostrils. A mouse's nose is made from a pointed part. Paint it grey, with a black tip. Add some thin strips of black card for the whiskers.

4

Make a small hole with a pencil either side of each nose. Tie a length of elastic to each nose and they are ready to wear! Which one do you like best?

45

Penguins

These penguins will look adorable in your bathroom!

You will need

Two egg boxes
White, black and pale blue paint
Yellow card
Six googly eyes

1

Cut three pointed parts from the base of an egg box.

2

Paint on a white tummy.

3

Paint the rest of the body black.

4

For the beak, cut out a triangle from a folded piece of yellow card. Glue in place.

5

Paint the base of an egg box to look like ice – your cute penguins can sit on it!

Pink Piglet

1

Cut off the end of an egg box. This will be the piglet's body.

2

Cut out one bowl and two pointed parts from the base of another egg box.

3

Glue a bowl to the front of the body. This is the snout. Glue the two pointed parts to the sides, to make the legs. Cut out two triangles from card, for ears. Glue in place.

4

Paint the piglet pink. Paint the nose and trotters darker pink.

5

Cut a strip of card and paint it light pink. Wrap it around a pencil, to make a curly tail.

6

Glue the tail in place. Cut out two circles from the card and paint them blue. Add them and the googly eyes to the piglet, as shown.

OINK
OINK

Robot

Robots at the ready! Make lots of these robots and you could create your own robot army!

You will need

Five egg boxes

Paints, including blue and white

White card

Two googly eyes

1

Paint an egg box blue. Add white, as shown, to make it look metallic. This is the body.

2

Cut four pointed parts from the bottom of another egg box. Paint them different colours.

3

Cut another egg box in half. Paint it light blue. This will be the head. Glue the head to the top of the body.

4

Cut the bowls from the base of another egg box. Glue two bowls together to make a barrel. Glue two barrels together to make two arms.

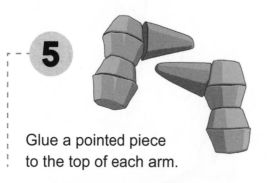

5

Glue a pointed piece to the top of each arm.

6

Use a pencil to make a hole in either side of the body, for the arms. Make two holes in the bottom, for the legs.

7

Glue the arms and legs in place.

8

Glue two bowls to the head and add some googly eyes. Cut a strip of card for the mouth, and glue on.

9

Cut the ends off the top of an egg box, and paint. Recycle the middle bit. Glue it to the bottom of the legs.

Handy Hint

Always allow the glue to dry completely before moving your model.

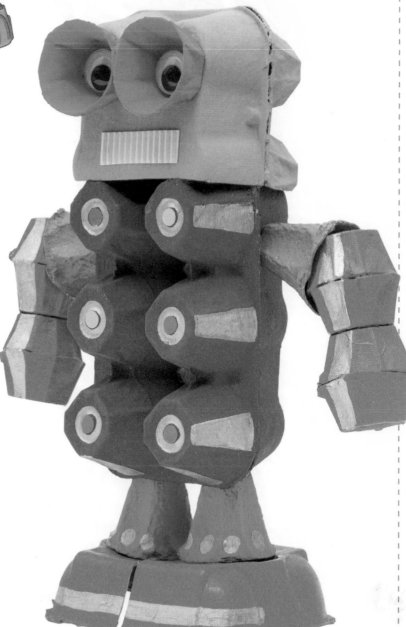

Rocket

5, 4, 3, 2, 1... Get ready for blast-off with this bright rocket.

You will need

Three egg boxes
Paint, including red and blue

1

Cut two pointed parts from the base of an egg box. Paint them red. Paint another egg box blue.

2

Use a pencil to make two holes in the end of the egg box. Insert the pointed parts and glue into position.

3

Cut off the corner of another egg box, to make a triangle.

4

Glue the triangle to the top of the egg box, and paint blue. Paint on some details, including windows and your cool rocket is ready to go!

WHOOSH

spider

You will need

One egg box
Black and pink paint
Card
Two googly eyes

1 Paint the bottom part of an egg box black.

2 Cut out eight legs from card, and paint black.

3 Bend each leg into a Z shape.

4 Glue the legs to the underside of the body.

5 Turn over the spider, and paint on some pink spots. Cut out circles from the card and paint them pink. Add them and the googly eyes, and find someone to scare!

Spotty Snake

Sssssssssssssssssssssss! This sensationally spotty snake is sssssso stunning you will want to make more than just one!

You will need

Four or more egg boxes
Paint
String
One straw
Red card
Two googly eyes

1

Cut the bowls from the base of the egg boxes. The more bowls you cut, the longer your snake will be.

2

Place two bowls together to make a barrel. Use all the bowls you cut to make lots of barrels.

3

Paint the barrels bright colours. Use a pencil to make a hole through both ends of the barrels.

4

Cut a pointed part from the base of an egg box. Paint it, and make a hole in the small end with a pencil.

5

Tie a knot in a long piece of string. Attach the string to a straw, then thread through all the barrels. Tie a knot in the end of the string.

SSSSSS

6

Cut a strip of red card. Cut a V in one end. This will be the tongue. Glue in place and add googly eyes. Your snake is ready to slither!

Handy Hint

Paint spots onto the barrels to make your snake really stand out.

Kangaroo

1

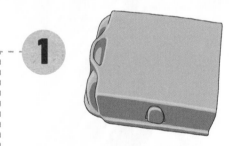

Cut off the end of an egg box.

2

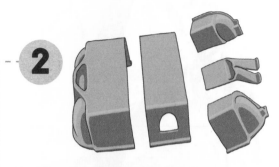

Cut the lid of another egg box into sections, as shown. The large piece will be a pouch. The small pieces will be feet.

3

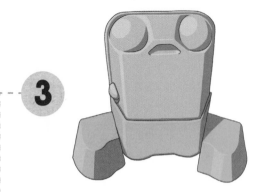

Glue the pouch to the front of the egg box. Glue the feet to the sides of the egg box, as shown.

4

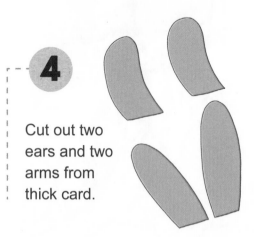

Cut out two ears and two arms from thick card.

5

Glue the ears and arms into position. Paint the body light brown, with a cream belly. Add some pink to the ears.

6

Cut a bowl from the base of an egg box. Cut out two small ears from thick card. Paint dark brown and pink.

7

Glue the baby kangaroo into the mother's pouch. Add a pair of card arms, as shown.

8

For the mother, place the googly eyes onto circles of green felt and glue into position. Glue the baby's eyes on too. Add noses and smiles.

Handy Hint

Not all kangaroos are reddish-brown, some are grey, so you could use grey paint, too.

Moustache Mask

No one will recognise you with this great disguise!

You will need

One egg box

Pink and black paint

Thick card

Elastic

1

Cut the end from the base of an egg box, as shown.

2

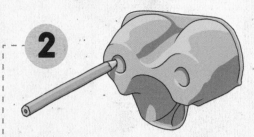

To make eyes, press a pencil into the egg box, as shown. Trim any rough edges.

3

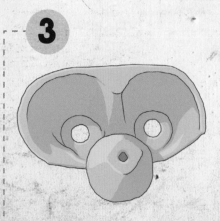

Paint your mask pink.

4

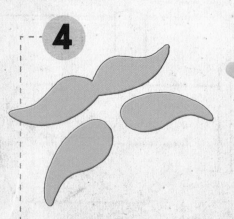

From thick card, cut out a moustache and a pair of eyebrows. Paint them black.

5

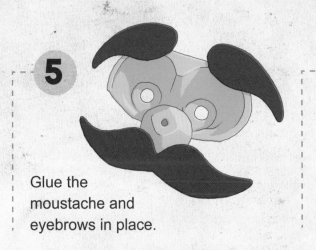

Glue the moustache and eyebrows in place.

6

On either side of the nose, make a hole with a pencil. Thread a piece of elastic through the holes. Tie a knot at each end to hold it in position. Now your disguise is ready!

TA DAH!

Mini Bugs

1

Cut three bowls from the base of an egg box.

Handy Hint
In nature, the brighter the colours, the deadlier the bug!

2

Paint the bowls bright colours.

3

Add spots or stripes.

4

Cut 18 narrow strips of black felt or card. Glue six to the inside of each bowl.

5

Add a pair of googly eyes to each bug and they're ready to scuttle away!

Pretty Fish

Turn your bedroom or bathroom into a sea world adventure zone with this pretty fish display.

You will need

Three egg boxes
Paint
Four straws
Ten googly eyes

1

Make five fish. For each, cut three bowls from an egg box.

2

Glue two of the bowls together, to make a barrel. Glue the other bowl to the top, to make the tail.

3

Cut a V-shaped notch in each tail. Paint the inside and outside different colours. Add some spots or stripes, a dot for a mouth and googly eyes.

4

Use a pencil to make a hole in the bottom of each fish. Insert the straws into the holes, and glue into position.

5

Paint the lid of an egg box and make some holes with a pencil. Insert the straws into the holes, and glue them into position.

59

Duckling

1

Cut three bowls and one pointed part from the base of an egg box.

2

Glue the two bowls together, to make a barrel. Then glue the pointed part to the top.

3

Glue the other bowl onto the pointed part. Paint all parts yellow.

4

Cut out two webbed feet and a bill from a piece of orange card. Glue the feet and bill into position.

5

Add two googly eyes and your duck is ready to quack, quack, quack!

Mouse Finger Puppet

You will need

Egg boxes

Grey or white, black and pink paint

Card

Two googly eyes

1 For the head, cut a pointed part from the base of an egg box.

2 Paint the part grey or white. Paint the end black.

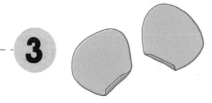

3 Cut out two ears from card. Paint them to match the head.

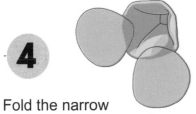

4 Fold the narrow ends of the ears, and glue to the inside of the head.

5 Paint the inside of the ears pink, and add a pair of googly eyes. Squeak!

Goggle Eyes

Amaze your friends with these incredible goggle eyes!

1 Cut two bowls from the base of an egg box.

2 Use a pencil to make a hole in the centre of the bowls. Trim any rough edges.

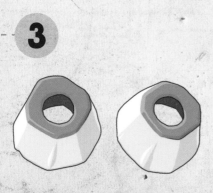

3 Paint the sides of the bowls white and the tops any eye colour you choose.

4 Cut two strips of black card. Cut slits along one edge. Glue to the tops of the bowls, for eyelashes.

5

Make a hole in each side of the bowls. Thread a short piece of elastic through the middle holes, as shown. Tie a knot at each end. Repeat using a longer piece of elastic for the other two holes on the outer edge. Your goggle eyes are ready to wear.

Handy Hint
You can add extra eyelashes to the bottom of your eyes, too!

Monster

Are there monsters in your bedroom? Scare them off with this happy little monster friend!

You will need

Three egg boxes
Paint
Three googly eyes

1

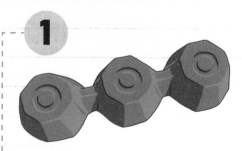

Cut a row of three bowls from the base of an egg box.

2

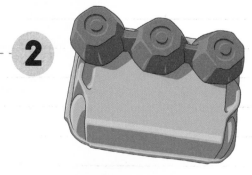

Glue the bowls onto another egg box to make the monster's body.

3

To make the feet, cut both ends off the lid of an egg box.

4

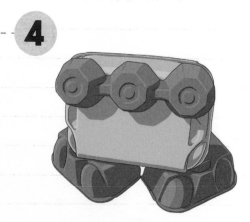

Glue the ends to the base of the monster's body.

5

Cut two pointed parts from the base of an egg box, for the horns. Paint the monster.

6

Paint on spots and claws, and three circles of pink. Glue googly eyes on top. Add a smile to this not-so-scary monster!

SO CUTE!

Crocodile

This snappy croc will keep guard outside your bedroom. Why not make another crocodile and let them snap at each other?

You will need

Four egg boxes
(one must have hinges on the short side)
Thick card
Green and yellow paint
Two googly eyes

1

Cut two bowls from the bottom of an egg box for the eyes.

2

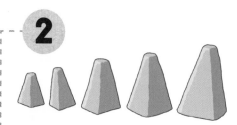

Cut about five pointed parts from the bottom of another egg box, for the spiky tail. Cut them into different sizes.

3

Place the short-side opening egg box upright, with another regular box next to it, upside-down. Arrange the tail spikes in a line, as shown. Cut a piece of thick card the same length as the crocodile.

4

Glue all the parts onto the thick card. Glue the eye pieces to the top of the head.

5

Paint the crocodile a bright green, with yellow spots. Add googly eyes.

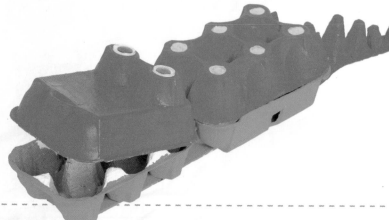

Witch

You will need

One egg box
Black paint
Polystyrene ball
Purple and black felt

1

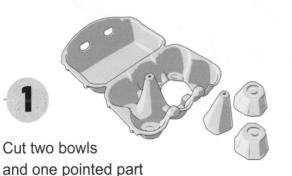

Cut two bowls and one pointed part from the base of an egg box.

2

Glue the two bowls together, to make a barrel. Paint all the parts black.

3

Paint a polystyrene ball yellow. Glue to the top of the barrel.

4

Cut a strip of purple felt. Make slits along one edge. Glue to the inside of the hat.

5

Cut a cape from some black felt and glue it to the body.

6

Draw on some features and make a pumpkin. You will need another barrel, orange paint, a green straw and felt.

Pirate Ship

Ahoy there, me hearties! Prepare to set sail on the seven seas with this awesome pirate ship – arrrrgh!

You will need

Two 12-egg boxes
One six-egg box
Brown, blue, black and red paint
Yellow and white card
Three straws

1

Glue the top of a long egg box onto another long egg box.

2

Glue a small egg box onto the top. Paint all boxes brown.

3

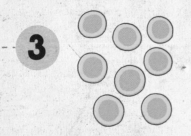

Cut out lots of yellow circles. Paint the middles pale blue. These will be the portholes.

4

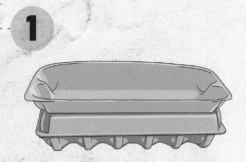

Glue the portholes into position.

5

From card, cut out five different-sized squares. Paint one with stripes and another with a skull and crossbones. These will be the ship's sails.

6

Use a pencil to make three holes along the top of the ship. Insert three straws into the holes for the masts, and glue into position.

7

Glue the sails to the straws before setting off on your next pirate adventure.

LAND AHOY!

Handy Hint

You can add some coloured card to make the ship's deck, too.

Plane

You could make lots of these cool little planes and hang them from your bedroom ceiling.

You will need

Two egg boxes
Paint, including blue
Card, including yellow
Split pin

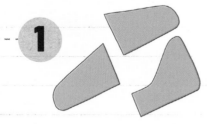

1 Cut out two wings and a tail from thick card.

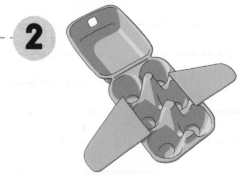

2 Glue the wings to the inside of an opened egg box.

3 Cut a slit in one end of the box, and glue the tail into position. Paint your plane.

4 Cut a bowl from another egg box, cut a notch in either side and paint the same colour as your plane. Cut a pointed part from the egg box. Cut four slits, flatten the part and paint a different colour. This will be the propeller for your plane.

5 Make a hole with pencil in the middle of the propeller and the bowl. Use a split pin to attach them, as shown.

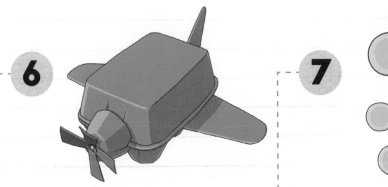

6

Glue the nose and propeller into position.

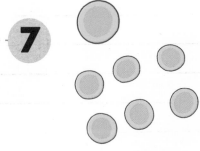

7

Cut out six small yellow circles and a large one. Paint the centres pale blue. Cut the large circle in half, to make windows for the front of the plane.

8

Glue the windows into position.

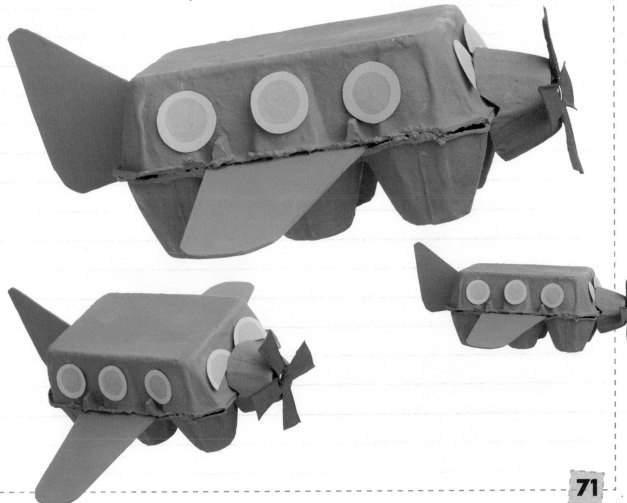

Treasure Chest

Nowhere to hide your lovely loot? Problem solved. Make this awesome treasure chest, then hide all your booty in it!

You will need

Three egg boxes
Brown and yellow paint
Yellow card
Ribbon for the treasure

1

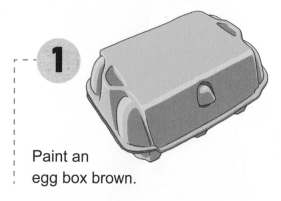

Paint an egg box brown.

2

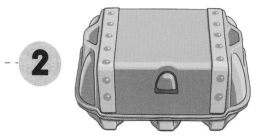

Cut two strips of yellow card and glue to the top of the box. Draw on some rivets with an orange pen.

3

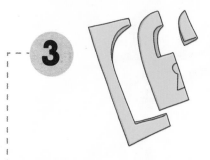

Fold a piece of yellow card in half, and cut out a padlock, as shown.

4

Draw on the keyhole with a black pen.

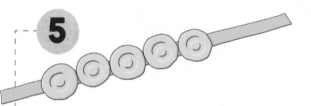

5

Cut out circles from the bases
of two more egg boxes. Glue
them to the ribbon to make
treasure, and paint yellow.

6

You can make necklaces
and gold, too. Keep it hidden
from any pirates, though!

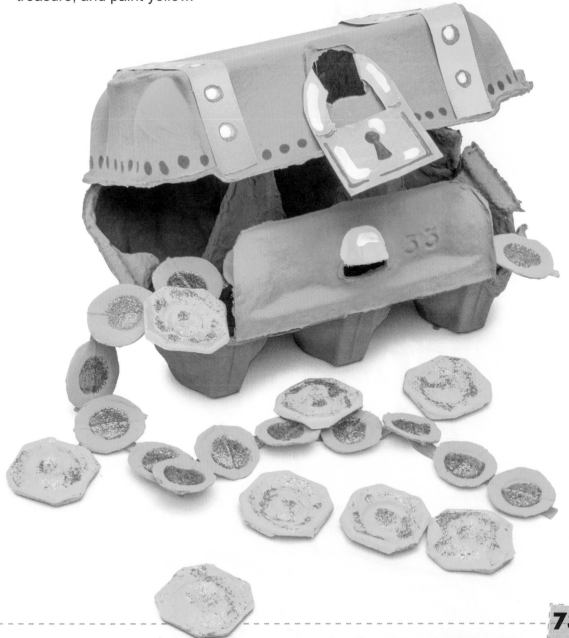

Tug Boat

This tug boat is so simple to make, you could make lots of them – and have plenty of time to play with them afterwards.

You will need

One 12-egg box
Two six-egg boxes
Paint
Yellow and grey card

1

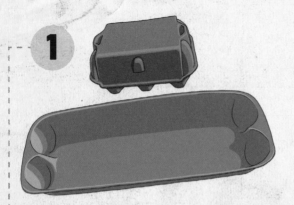

Cut the top off a long egg box, and paint it. Paint a small egg box a different colour.

2

Glue the small egg box onto the middle of the long box.

3

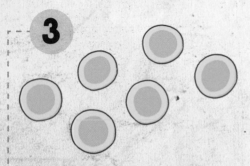

Cut out lots of yellow circles. Paint the centres pale blue. These will be the portholes.

CHUG CHUG

4

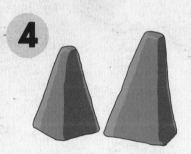

Cut two pointed parts from the base of an egg box, and paint. These will be the funnels.

5

Use a pencil to make two holes along the top of the boat. Insert the funnels and glue into position.

6

Cut out a cloud shape from grey card. Make a slit in the bottom, and slot onto one of funnels, for billowing smoke. Your tug boat is now ready to go to work!

Tractor

Brrrm, beep, beep! Life on a farm is busy, so get ready to make this hard-working tractor, then put it to work!

1

Cut two lids from egg boxes, and glue together to make the body of the tractor.

2

Cut another box in half and glue the bottom edges together to make the cab.

3

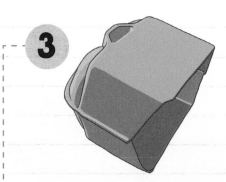

Cut a V-shaped notch in the bottom of the cab.

4

Glue the cab to the body, as shown, and paint them red.

5

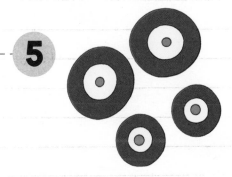

Cut out two large and two
small circles from thick card.
Paint them to look like wheels.

6

Glue the wheels
to the tractor body.

7

Add some windows and
a shiny grill made from
corrugated card so your
tractor can chug, chug along!

Cute Crab

This cheeky little crab will look lovely in a bathroom or with other sea creatures.

You will need

Two egg boxes
Card
Paint
Two split pins
Two googly eyes

1 Cut two bowls from the base of an egg box.

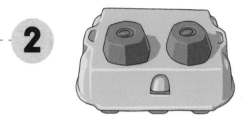

2 Glue the bowls to the top of another box, for the eyes.

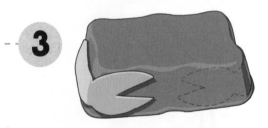

3 From card, cut two claws. Make sure they are large enough to fit around your crab's body, as shown.

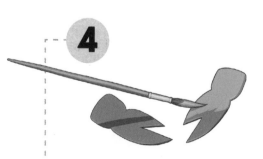

4 Now paint the claws.

5 Paint crab's body, and add some spots to its shell.

6

Use a pencil to push a hole through the claw and shell of the crab. Attach each claw to the body with a split pin.

Handy Hint
Make the holes in step 6 smaller than the head of the split pin.

7

Add some googly eyes. Your crab is now ready, but be careful it doesn't nip you!

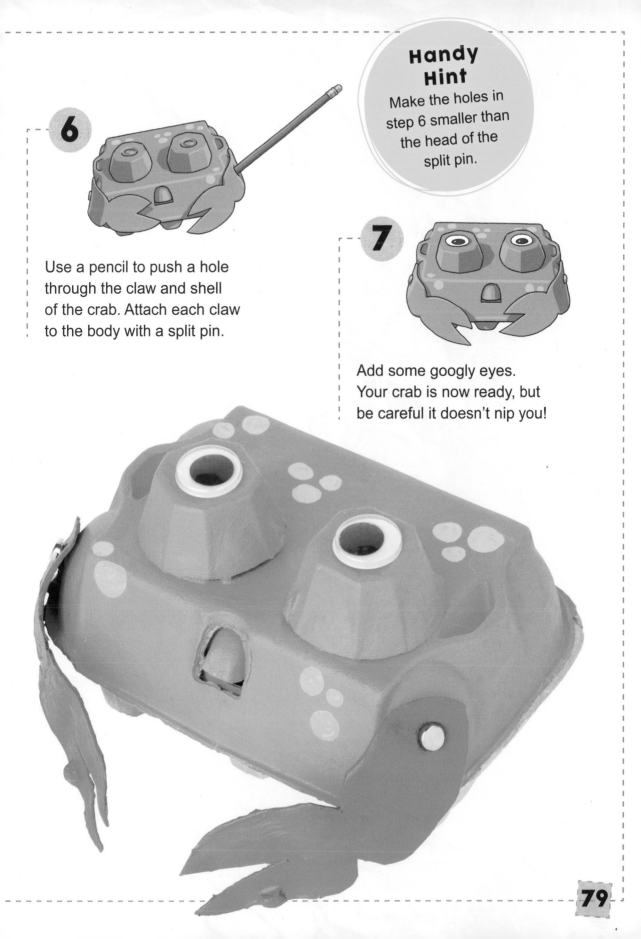

Quarto is the authority on a wide range of topics.

Quarto educates, entertains and enriches the lives of our readers—enthusiasts and lovers of hands-on living.

www.quartoknows.com

Publisher: Maxime Boucknooghe
Editorial Director: Victoria Garrard
Art Director: Miranda Snow
Editors: Sophie Hallam, Sarah Eason and Jennifer Sanderson
Designer: Paul Myerscough
Photographer: Michael Wicks
Illustrator: Tom Connell
With thanks to our wonderful models Islah, Ethan and Ania.

First published in the UK in 2016
by QED Publishing
Part of The Quarto Group
The Old Brewery, 6 Blundell Street
London, N7 9BH

A catalogue record for this book is available from the British Library.

ISBN 978 1 78493 557 3

Printed in China